Indian Games and Crafts

INDIAN GAMES

GRAY-WOLF

New York   William Morro

AND CRAFTS

WRITTEN AND ILLUSTRATED BY

ROBERT HOFSINDE

(Gray-Wolf)

and Company   1957

To the memory of
my mother,
who taught me to use
my hands.

By the same author:

INDIAN SIGN LANGUAGE

THE INDIAN'S SECRET WORLD

Contents

1

Guessing Game

THIS game was a great time-passer among the Plains Indians. For yourself and your friends it can become a good rainy-day activity, easy to make and fun to play, and the necessary materials cost very little.

Eight sticks, each 12 inches long and ¼ inch in diameter.

India ink and a brush.

Coping saw.

Pocketknife.

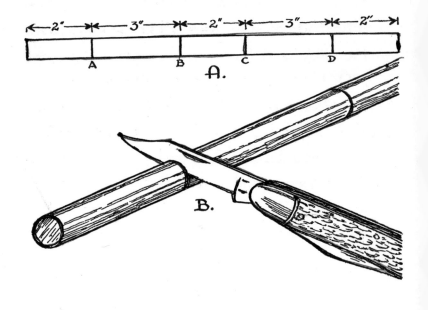

There are two ways to make the eight sticks. The Indian way is to select eight fairly straight branches of the proper size, preferably willow. Cut the ends of the sticks off straight and even. Use either the knife or the coping saw. On each stick mark off 5 sections, using the dimensions shown in A. With the small blade of a sharp knife, cut into the bark in a straight line around the stick at points A, B, C, D, as shown in B. Four such cuts must be made on each stick. Hold the knife blade on the stick, and then roll the stick away from you. This will cut the bark through to the inner wood. After the cuts have been made, use the point of the blade, as in C, to peel away the thin bark between the cuts. The bark should be peeled away between A and B, and between C and D— shown in D. Fix seven sticks in this manner. On the eighth stick leave the bark strip between B

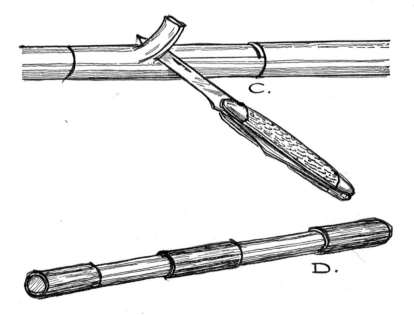

C.

D.

and c, and peel off the rest of the bark clear to the ends, as in E.

The white man's way of preparing the sticks is better if you live in a town or city where branches are hard to obtain. In this case, use dowel sticks, ¼ inch thick by 12 inches long. Lumberyards and most hardware stores have them in stock, and they are inexpensive.

With a pencil, mark off the same dimensions as for the peeled sticks, and then paint the two-inch

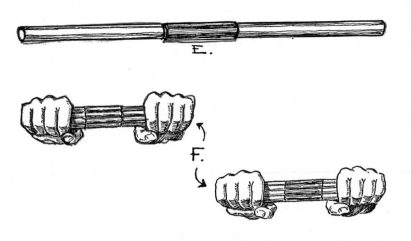

E.

F.

sections with India ink to take the place of the bark. This type of ink is suggested because it dries quickly and is waterproof. It will not rub off on your hands when you handle the sticks.

Two teams with four to eight on each side can play this game. They are seated on the ground so that the teams face each other, and a folded robe or blanket is placed between them.

One team holds the sticks. Hiding them under the blanket, two teammates divide the eight sticks into two bundles of four each. These two players then grasp the two bundles in such a manner that the painted ends are covered by their hands, as shown in F. They then hold out the bundles of sticks toward their opponents.

The object of the game is for the other team to guess in which of the two bundles the odd stick is hidden. As all the eight sticks have a center marking, it is no easy task.

If the rival team misses its guess, the first team gets one point. It shuffles the sticks again under the blanket, and the next two players grasp the bundles and hold them forward.

If, on the other hand, the opponents guess right, then it is their turn to hold the sticks, and the first team must guess.

Each team may keep its own score, or a scorekeeper may be appointed. The scorekeeper sits between the teams, at one end of the folded blanket.

Colored toothpicks can be used for keeping score. One team is indicated by red, and the other by green toothpicks. The scorekeeper holds 20 of each color. When a member of a team guesses correctly, the scorekeeper places a toothpick belonging to that team in front of him. The members of each team take turns guessing. The team whose 20 toothpicks are first used up is the winning team.

2

Bowl Game

THE rain was pelting down on the skin covering of the tepee, but a group of Crow Indians sat snug within, playing the bowl game around a small fire made of buffalo chips.

One player held a small wooden bowl in his hand. As the others looked on, he tossed into the air a number of peach pits that were in the bowl. Then he skillfully caught them in the bowl again. The men were divided into two teams, and both teams watched closely to see how the stones landed and how the play was scored. Both sides wanted to win, for each man on the winning side would be given a pony by the losers.

To play the game with your friends, you need the following equipment:

One small salad bowl of turned wood or a small woven breadbasket. Either can be bought in a five-and-ten-cent store.

Six peach or plum pits.

A small bottle of India ink.

A pen point and holder.

Any even number of people can play this game, even as few as two. It is more exciting if there are three or four players, or even more, on each team.

Wash the pits and let them dry thoroughly.

Then, with the pen and ink, draw a broad line across one side of each stone, as in A. Drop the six pits into the bowl, B, or the basket, C. Hold the bowl in one hand and, with a slight toss, flip the pits up into the air, and catch them again in the bowl. Score by counting the number of pits that land with the marked side up. Each one that

A.

B.

C.

lands with the marked side up counts one point. After scoring your turn, pass the bowl over to your opponent. He makes a toss, counts his score, and passes the bowl back to you.

Each player keeps his own score with toothpicks. The winner is the one having the most toothpicks in front of him after twenty tosses.

If as many as six are playing the game, divide up into two teams, facing each other, with three players on each team. The first man on your team makes the first toss and counts his score. He then passes the bowl to the opponent directly opposite him. The opponent tosses, counts his score, and the bowl goes to the second man on your team.

Usually each man keeps score of his own toss, but an official scorekeeper may be appointed. At the end of a game of ten tosses by each player, the final team scores are tallied, and the team with the largest score wins.

This bowl game was played by nearly every tribe in the country. The Plains and Woodland

GRAY-WOLF.

Indians used a wooden bowl for the game. The Indians of the Southwest more often used a fine, woven basket.

The game can be played for marbles, arrowheads, or gumdrops. Then the losing team hands over one marble, for example, for each point won by the other team. The winnings are then divided among the players whose team has won.

3

Zuñi Kick Stick

IT WAS a festive day in the Zuñi village, for the prayers and dances of the people had been answered. Rain had come at last the day before, to water the crops and settle the dry, swirling dust on the plaza.

In the center of the plaza a stout stick had been set into the ground. Now an Indian tied a long, braided rawhide lariat to the stick. He stretched out the lariat as far as it would go, about thirty feet, and tied another stick to the free end. Then, making sure to keep the lariat taut, he walked backwards and, with the end of the stick, scratched a deep circular groove in the hard-packed earth. Another Indian followed him and made the circle visible to everyone by sprinkling white corn meal in the groove.

When the circle was finished, two officials stepped into its center. Each held up a stick about 12 inches long. Each stick was carved and decorated in a different pattern. Together the of-

ficials called for contestants. The people teased and joked and called out the names of friends and relatives. Then a roar of laughter went up as two old men, each almost ninety years old, stepped into the circle.

The two officials greeted them ceremoniously and with much head shaking told them that they were too young. As the two old men walked away, two young Zuñi men stepped into the ring. A hush came over the crowd.

One official walked to the edge of the circle and drew a line on the ground with his foot. The contestants took their places on the line, and in front of each one the officials placed one of the carved sticks. One official gave a quick spoken signal, and the young men began kicking their sticks ahead, making sure not to kick them outside of the circle. The spectators shouted encouragement as the players rounded the circle and came back toward the starting line. Then one swift kick sent a stick over the line, and the player dashed after it. He was the winner.

Kick stick is still played among the Zuñi In-

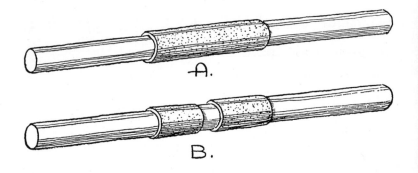

-A.

B.

dians, and it is a very useful game to know. Around the fire in a summer camp, for instance, the campers may sit in a large circle to make the ring, and the kick sticks can be made in a few minutes. Simply take two straight branches, each about 12 inches long and 1 inch thick, and of approximately equal weight. Peel each stick with a pocketknife, leaving a 2-inch strip of bark in the center. To tell the sticks apart, peel a ¼-inch slice from the center of one bark strip. See A and B. Now draw a starting line within the council ring in front of the chief's seat.

If, on his way around, a player kicks his stick out of the circle, or if it touches a spectator, the player is disqualified. The other player must continue, however, for if he should also kick out of the circle, then there is no game, and the players must start over.

In planning ahead for a games night in camp, where other games described in this book can be played, you can make permanent kick sticks out of two birch dowel rods of the same size as the branches. To tell the dowels apart, paint one red and one green, or else paint each with a different-colored band.

4

Corncob Darts

AUGUST, the Green Corn Moon, had come once again, and the boys of the Chippewa Village had obtained their mothers' permission to gather two ears apiece of the new green corn.

The boys had swarmed over the cornfield like so many blackbirds over a berry bush, and now they were all gathered on the shady side of Two Arrows' wigwam. Quick brown hands darted from corn to bone awl to feathers, as each boy worked on making his darts.

26

The husks were peeled away, and the kernels shelled off. Then, with a sharp bone awl, four holes were drilled into the blunt end of each corncob. Four wild turkey feathers were inserted in these holes so that the tips of the feathers curved away from the center.

While all this activity was going on, one of the boys made a target. On a thick, flat piece of birch bark he scratched circles with a sharp stone. Then he peeled the bark away so that the dark inner bark showed in the center spot and in the third ring.

As soon as everything was in readiness, the group went to a fairly level clearing near the lake. Here the target was placed flat upon the ground; and a stick, cut to a point at one end, was driven through the center of the target and into the ground. The target was then lying flat on the ground, held firmly in place by the stick driven through it.

Drawing a line on the ground some twenty feet from the target, each boy in turn stepped up to this line, toed the mark, and hurled his corncob dart at the target. A scorekeeper kept the score on each throw.

Your own game of corncob darts is to be played in the same way, but your method of making the darts and the target will differ a little. Here are the materials you will need:

Several ears of fresh corn, green if you can obtain them.

Chicken or turkey feathers.

One small awl or an ice pick.

Small tube of gluing cement.

Pocketknife.

One piece of plywood, 26 inches square and ½ inch thick.

One piece of wood, 1 inch square by 4 inches long.

One thin screw, 1 inch long.

Screw driver.

Four small jars of poster colors—one each of red, blue, white, and yellow.

A small water-color brush.

Pull the husks off the corn. Grasp the ear firmly with the left hand; a rotary motion with the right

A.

B.

hand around the corn will shell off the kernels, leaving you the bare cob. The corn must not be cooked; boiling it will leave the cob soft and useless for darts.

With a sharp knife, cut the top of the cob across evenly. With the awl or ice pick, punch four holes into the end of the cob, as in A. Drop a little gluing cement into the holes, and insert the four feathers in such a manner that the feathers curve outward, as in B. The making of the dart takes only a few minutes. There should be 2 darts, if possible, for each player.

Now comes the target. This is made from the 26-inch piece of plywood. First determine the exact center of the board. To do this, draw a line across the board from one corner to the other. Then draw another line across, connecting the other two corners. The point where these two lines intersect is the center. To draw the circle, place a small nail in the center of the board, C. To this fasten a cord about 14 inches long. Tie a pencil at the end of the cord exactly 13 inches from the nail. Holding the pencil straight up and down, draw the circle. Cut with a coping saw along this line and you have a circular target.

After the target has been cut, place the nail in the center again and tie the string to it. Tie the

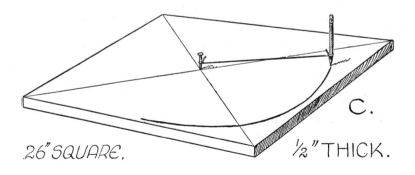

26" SQUARE. C. ½"THICK.

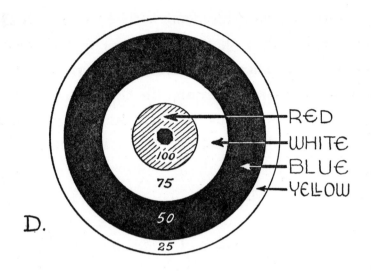

RED
WHITE
BLUE
YELLOW

100
75
50
25

D.

pencil 1½ inches from the nail and draw the center spot. Tie the pencil 5 inches from the nail and draw the small red circle. Tie the pencil 8½ inches from the nail for the white circle, and 12 inches from the nail for the blue, which will leave one inch for the final, or yellow, circle. Paint the circles as indicated in D, using poster colors. When the paint is dry, add the score numbers as shown: add the numerals 100, 75, and 25 with blue paint; add the numeral 50 in white paint. See D.

Next trim the edges from the 1-by-4-inch piece of wood with a sharp knife, making the piece eight-sided. Then drive the small nail used for making the circles through the target so the center can be seen from the back. Insert the 1-inch screw through this hole in the target and up into the center of the 4-inch piece of wood. Then paint this piece of wood red. See E.

To play the game, place the target on the ground or on the floor, if indoors, and mark off a line fifteen to twenty feet from the target. See

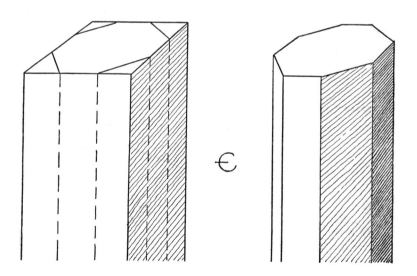

F. The player toes the mark and throws the dart from that position. The ring on which the dart comes to rest is counted as the score. If the dart rests across two colors, then the color covered by the greatest part of the dart is counted.

Score with the following counts:

Red center spot, 100 points.
White, 75.
Blue, 50.
Yellow, 25.

As soon as the play is scored, the player picks up his dart, and the next player takes his turn.

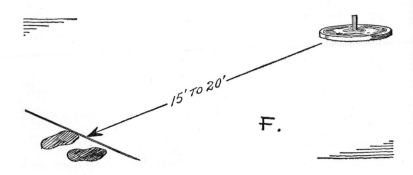

5

Eskimo Buzz Board

DURING the long sunless period in the far
north, Eskimo children amuse themselves with
their carved buzz boards. Actually, this is not a
game you will want to play, but it is a toy that
younger children will enjoy and that you will find
interesting to make.

The buzz boards made by the Eskimos are often carved from ivory, but sometimes driftwood
is the material used. However, since it would
probably be difficult for you to obtain ivory, we

can make our board out of wood. Here is what you will need:

One piece of wood, white pine or plywood, 2½ inches by 3½ inches by ¼ inch thick.

Fine-grained sandpaper.

Coping saw.

Red and black water colors from your paintbox.

A small water-color brush.

A pump drill, see Chapter 13, or a small hand drill.

One piece of strong, thin cord, 40 inches long.

Paper and pencil.

Mark off on paper the ¼-inch squares shown in A—14 squares one way, and 10 the other. Within the squares draw the outline of the buzz board and the designs. Rub the entire back of the drawing with a soft black pencil.

Sandpaper the piece of wood until it is smooth; then place the blackened side of the drawing upon the wood, and trace it over, transferring the drawing to the wood.

With the coping saw cut the outlines of the

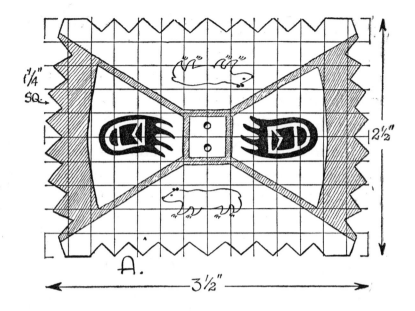

A.

¼" sq.

2½"

3½"

board, taking care that the notches are all even, and then paint the design on one side. Use black paint where the drawing is black. Use red in the shaded areas. The white in the drawing is the natural wood showing between the painted parts of the design.

If you have a wood-burning set, you may burn these designs into the wood instead of painting them.

See B for drawings that can be used on the other side of the board in place of the polar bear; the central design with the bear paws can be reversed in coloring; that is, you can make the paws red and the shaded areas black.

In the middle of the board, above and below the exact center, make two small holes through the wood with your drill. Pass the 40-inch cord

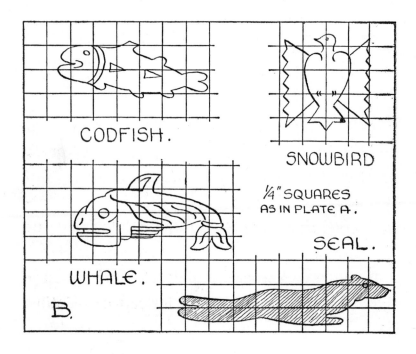

CODFISH.

SNOWBIRD

¼" SQUARES
AS IN PLATE A.

SEAL.

WHALE.

B.

through these two holes and knot the ends together, as in C.

Grasping the loops of string in the manner shown in the drawing, first pull the cord tight and then release it; pull it again, then release it. Do this in quick succession, and the board will spin and whirl and buzz. The faster you work it, the more noise it will make.

KNOT DETAIL.

C.

6

Toss Ball

HERE is a simple Indian game that is great fun to play. Show your friends the ball, and ask them how far they think they can throw it—while lying flat on their backs. Watch their expressions as they discover that they cannot toss the ball nearly as far as they thought they could.

First of all, you will need a ball. An old tennis ball that has lost its bounce will do nicely. With an awl or an ice pick, poke two holes in the ball, close together on one side. See A. Then pinch up

A.

the ball so that you can pass a strong cord 10 inches long or a shoelace cut to the same length through both holes, as in A. Now tie a knot in the cord close to the ball, so that the cord will not slip, and then tie the ends of the cord together to form a loop. See B.

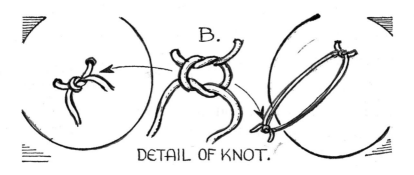

B.

DETAIL OF KNOT.

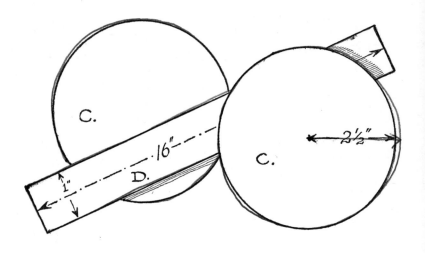

If you would like to make a ball similar to the buckskin ball actually used by the Indians, follow patterns C-C and D. A piece of chamois, in place of buckskin, can be bought at the five-and-ten-cent store or a drugstore.

Make a pattern of the circle and the strip with the dimensions shown in C and D. First draw it on heavy paper. Then cut out the patterns and trace them on your material. Trace the round pattern twice, so that you will have two matching circles. When you have finished, cut the three pieces out carefully with a pair of scissors.

After the three pieces are cut, tie in the loop cord, as shown in E, by making two small holes in the center of one circle. Pass a cord through the holes and through a button on the other side and knot the ends of the cord to form a loop. When you sew the cover together, the button should be on the inside and the knot on the outside. See E, F, and G.

Now sew one of the circles to the long edge of the one-inch strip, using the stitch shown in F and G. This is known as the squaw stitch, because most Indian women used it in sewing two pieces of buckskin together. It leaves no inner seam.

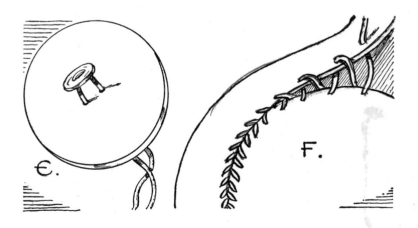

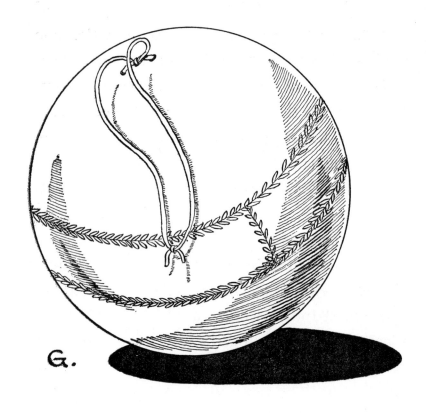

G.

When this sewing is completed, stitch the ends of the strip together, and sew the other circle of leather to the second side of the strip. This circle should only be stitched together part of the way around, in order to leave an opening through which the ball can be stuffed.

Cotton, excelsior, and even grass make fine stuffing, as they can be packed firmly and molded to shape. Stuff the ball as tightly as possible, shaping it to a firm roundness as you work, and finally, when it can hold no more, sew up the remaining opening.

Get together with some of your friends and play the game. First, scratch a straight line in the dirt with a stick. Each player in turn must place himself flat on his back, with his shoulders resting on the line. He grasps the loop cord on the ball, swings his arm up and over his head, and throws the ball behind him as far as he can.

The spot where the ball lands is marked with a stick or a stone or an owner stick. (See Chapter 12.) Then the next player takes his turn.

Remember; it is where the ball *first* hits the ground that counts, not where it stops after rolling. Naturally, the player who throws the farthest is the winner.

7

Snow Snake

DURING the night a fine snow had fallen, hiding yesterday's tracks, and in the early morning sun this white blanket shimmered like millions of diamonds. The air was crisp, and as soon as the Iroquois Indian boys had finished their morning meal, they took up their snow snakes and hurried down to the frozen lake.

They planted the snow snakes upright in the snow and spread out in two long lines. Then, using wide strips of bark for shovels, they built up a long, narrow bank of snow in a straight line. It was about 2 feet high, and 3 feet wide, and 1000 to 2000 feet long.

While the rest of the boys flattened the top of this snowbank, two of them hurried into the nearby forest. Soon they returned with a fairly stout limb from a tree. Two branches were protruding from the thinner end. Taking hold of these branches, and walking one on each side of the snowbank, they dragged the limb along the top center of the bank, from one end to the other. The weight of the limb made a shallow trench in the snow, and by the time they reached the end, all the other boys were ready with their snow snakes.

Some of them rubbed snow on the belly side of the snakes; others had already poured water on theirs. This had frozen as soon as they stepped outdoors and would give added speed to the snow snakes when they were thrown.

Standing at one end of the prepared snowbank, each player in turn sent his snake skimming along the groove on top. Each player marked the place where his snake stopped, either with one of his arrows or with an owner stick. (See Chapter 12.)

Indians have been known to hurl their snow snakes at a speed of more than one hundred and twenty miles per hour, and to cover a distance of more than one mile. This interesting game was the national game of the Iroquois tribes.

However, for your own playing of the game, a snowbank, either on land or on good solid ice, need not be more than six to eight hundred yards long. But before you and your friends can play you will have to make the snow snakes, and this is what you will need in tools and materials:

One hickory or ash stave, 1¼ inches square and 5 feet long. Pine will do if that is the only wood you can get. Your local lumber dealer should have this.

A sharp pocketknife.

Rough and fine sandpaper from the five-and-ten-cent store.

Three ten-cent jars of poster colors, white, light green, dark green.

One small water-color brush.

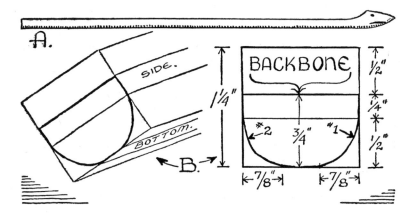

One small can of clear varnish, also from the five-and-ten.

One flat, ½-inch brush for the varnish.

One 1-inch bolt, ¼ inch thick. Ask the garage man for one.

One ½-inch drill.

Two roundheaded upholstery tacks for snake eyes.

To make the snow snake shown in A, mark off on your wooden stave the dimensions shown in B. Mark them first on the two sides numbered 1 and 2, then on the rounded lines from end to end of the stave, as indicated.

Draw the outline of the head and the flat back, both top and side views, as shown in C.

To hold the stave for carving, place it on a workbench or on a rough board, holding it in place by nailing a short crosspiece to the board at each end of the stave. This is shown in D.

Carve *with* the grain. Working with and against the grain is clearly shown in the drawings marked E.

Starting along the angular edges of the stave, trim off thin slivers, a little at a time, with your knife. Do not try to take the whole edge down to the line all at one time. If you own a small plane, this could be used instead of the knife.

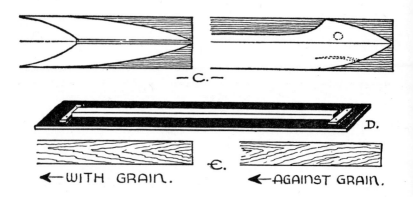

— C. —

D.

E.

◄—WITH GRAIN.   ◄—AGAINST GRAIN.

Repeat this carving on the other side. If it is done slowly and carefully, the belly side of the snake will finally be smoothly rounded.

While the stave still rests between the blocks, wrap a piece of coarse sandpaper around a small block of wood and sand the rounded sides, removing all roughness. Then polish the sides and belly with fine-grained sandpaper.

Now turn the stave over and, as shown in F, whittle the excess wood away from the back of the head and all the way down the straight part of the flat back. Remove layer after layer, as demonstrated in G.

The next step is to form the snake's head. Start

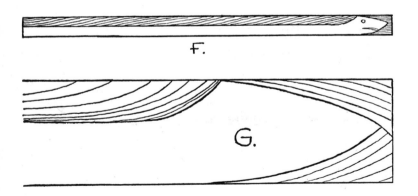

F.

G.

by shaping the top and then the bottom of the head. Finally taper the sides of the head toward the nose, leaving just a very narrow strip along the top of the head. The shaded areas shown in C and F are to be cut away.

The head and flat back must also be given a good sandpapering, first with coarse sandpaper and then with fine. The sandpaper on a block is to be used when sandpapering the back. If you hold the block straight, it will prevent you from rounding the edges.

Indian decorations should be added along the snow snake's back. Diagram H shows a simple but typical design. Draw up the squares as indicated on a strip of paper, and sketch in the design on your squares. Blacken the other side of the paper with a soft pencil. Place the blackened side of the paper against the wood. Starting near the head, transfer the design to the snake by tracing it.

This design is drawn so that when one tracing has been completed, you move the design down flush with the one above, and trace it again. The

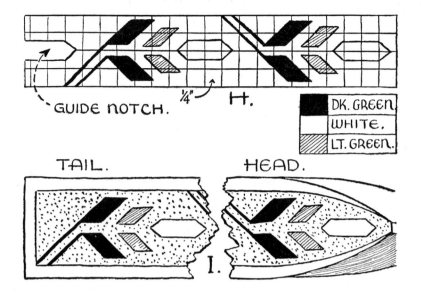

GUIDE NOTCH.   ¼"   H.

	DK. GREEN.
	WHITE.
	LT. GREEN.

TAIL.   HEAD.

I.

design is repeated down to the tip of the tail.

The design should then be painted in with the poster colors from the small jars. Three colors are indicated in H, but two colors may be used instead of three. The entire snow snake should then be varnished. If you own a wood-burning set, the design can be burned in, instead of painted, and then varnished. The dots shown in I should be burned in with the tip of the iron.

To make it possible to varnish the snake on all sides at one time, a small screw eye can be fastened to the tail end, and the snake can then be hung from a nail.

To make the snow snake waterproof and warpproof, three thin coats of the varnish are better than one thick coat.

The Indians prepared the playing field in either of two ways. To play on the ice of a frozen lake,

as we have learned, they took bark slabs and used them as shovels to build up a snowbank. See J. On land, or where the snow was deeper, the Indians used a different method. They tied a rope of braided rawhide to one end of a short log, about six inches thick and three or four feet long. Then one man made a shallow trough by dragging the log in a straight line through the snow, as shown in K.

K.

G.W.

If the head of the snow snake seems too light in weight, use a ½-inch bit to drill a hole at an angle into the back of the snake head, shown in L, and insert a short, thick bolt, ½ inch thick.

The finishing touches on the snake are the eyes and the mouth. Insert the two roundheaded upholstery nails for the eyes, and cut the mouth in a V-shape, using the small blade of the pocketknife. Both are shown in M.

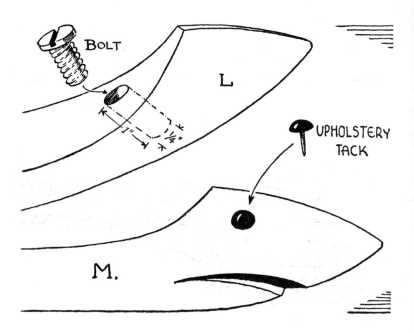

The snow snake can be thrown underhand, as in N, or overhand, as in O. The winning player, of course, is the one who can throw it the farthest.

You can build up a fine team by getting your friends interested in making their own snow snakes. To score in the Indian manner, use the

O.

owner sticks described in Chapter 12. When a player's snow snake stops sliding, insert the owner stick at the side of the trough on a line with the tip of the snow snake's nose.

8

Bull Roarer or Moaning Stick

THIS is an Indian noisemaker, and it was big medicine with several different Indian tribes. The Apache, Navaho, Ute, and Pueblo Indians lived on hot, dusty plains where there was little rain. When the sun threatened to destroy the crops, the tribe's medicine man would use the bull roarer to imitate the sound of onrushing wind. He hoped that the sound might call forth winds that would drive rain clouds over the parched fields and water them.

To add to their power, lightning symbols and thunderbird designs were painted on the flat sides of the moaning sticks. The Apache liked to make their sticks out of pine wood, particularly from a tree that had been struck by lightning. This wood, they believed, had even greater medicine power in producing a thunderstorm, since lightning had made its home in the tree.

The name *moaning stick* comes from the Sioux Indians. Sioux medicine men spun their sticks rapidly, making a loud, moaning sound; during funerals it was meant to drive off evil spirits.

To make your own bull roarer, the best wood to use is pine. If you follow the directions, your stick will hum loudly enough even without having been struck by lightning. You can get a piece of scrap wood from a lumberyard, or else use the endpiece of an orange or apple crate that your local grocer will give you. Here are the materials you will need:

Piece of wood, 8 inches long, 3 inches wide, ¼ inch thick.

Thin, strong string, 20 inches long.

Stick or dowel rod, ½ inch thick and 9 inches long for handle.

Small paintbrush.

Water colors.

Coping saw.

Pocketknife.

Both rough and fine sandpaper.

Small hand drill. (You can make and use the pump drill described in Chapter 13.)

For shape, size, and design, square off on a piece of paper the same number of ¼-inch squares as in A. If you have graph paper with ¼-inch squares, that can be used. Within these squares copy the shape of the bull roarer and the thunderbird design. Draw this with a regular pencil. Then draw the lightning design on the reverse side of the bull roarer.

When the roarer is cut out, wrap a piece of rough sandpaper around a block of wood, holding it in place with two thumbtacks, and sandpaper both sides of the wood and all edges.

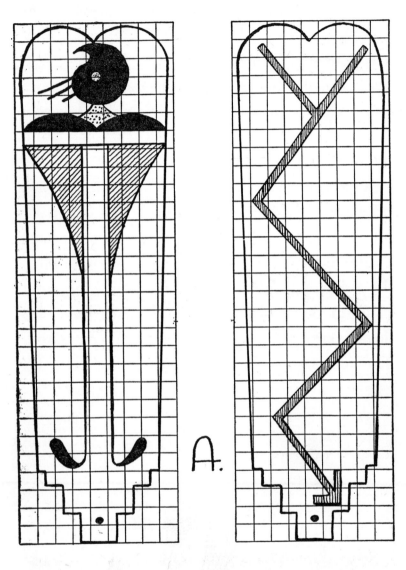

A.

Now rub the entire back of the drawing with a soft pencil, lay the design on the wood, and trace it over, transferring the design to the wood. Cut out the outline carefully with the coping saw.

If the wood used for the roarer has a nice grain, then the designs can be traced directly on the sanded surface. If not, paint the whole bull roarer bright blue with water-color paint. That will make a nice background for the design.

In either case, when you paint the thunderbird, the following colors should be used: the solid black in the drawing should be dark blue; the dotted portions, yellow; and the shaded parts, red. The lightning on the reverse side should be a zig-zag line in bright orange.

Near one end of your dowel cut a groove with your pocketknife, as in B. This will make the handle.

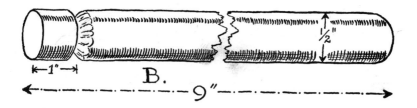

When the paint on the bull roarer is dry, drill a small hole near the bottom of the narrow end. Into this tie one end of the 20-inch string, making a slipknot, as shown in C and D.

Tie the other end of the string to the groove in the handle, with another slipknot, plus an extra knot, as in E. Be careful to tie these two knots so that the loop is loose enough to turn freely

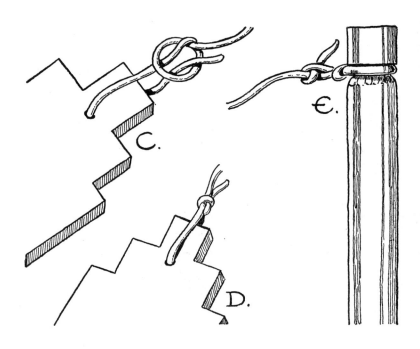

in the groove when the bull roarer is spinning.

Grasping the handle in your right hand, start spinning the bull roarer over your head. The faster you spin it, the louder it will moan.

As no two ever sound exactly alike, get your friends to make their own bull roarers, and then spin them all in unison. You will be surprised at how much noise you will make.

9

Double Ball and Stick

THE Iroquois village was deserted this afternoon. Just outside the stockade, the teams of the Wolf and Beaver clans were facing each other in the center of a large playing field. The spectators stood in deep silence on the side lines. The score was tied, and a single goal would decide the winner of this hard, swift game of double ball.

The umpire, a warrior named Swift Eagle from the Turtle clan, waited until the teams were ready.

Then suddenly he threw the double ball into the air between the teams, and at once there was a mad scramble of men and sticks. A Beaver man caught the thong between the balls with his crooked stick. Dodging right and left, he managed to get past the men of the Wolf team. When he had gained a lead, he stopped short. With a sure aim he sent the double ball flying through the air toward the Wolf goal. In a flash it had reached the goal, and the thong caught neatly on the crossbar of the goal posts.

Swift Eagle moved the scoring sticks together. The game was over, and the Beaver team had won. That night the Wolf clan gave a feast for their friends from the Beaver clan.

This game was played in spring, summer, and fall. Actually, it was more of a women's game, but the men played it from time to time. Played by either group, double ball was hard and fast.

You can play this exciting game, and you and your friends can make the double ball and sticks by following the instructions below. Here are the materials and tools you will need:

One piece of chamois skin, 8 inches by 12 inches. May be bought in five-and-ten-cent store or drugstore.

One spool of No. 8 thread.

One large-eyed needle.

Scissors.

Coping saw.

Pocketknife.

Paper and pencil.

Cotton.

The lid from an instant-coffee jar or some other small jar. The diameter should be about 2¼ inches.

A piece of plywood, 4 x 16 inches, and ¾ inch thick.

One dowel rod, 12 inches long, ½ inch thick.

First draw a paper pattern for the double ball. Measure off a rectangle 2¼ inches wide and 5 inches high. See A. Place the jar lid on the paper within the measurements, so that the jar edge touches the top line and the two side lines. Outline the lid, holding your pencil straight up and down in order to make your circle accurate.

Now move the lid down so that the rim touches

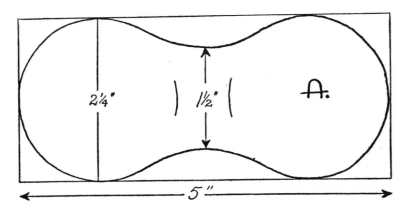

CUT 4, 2 FOR EACH DOUBLE BALL

the bottom and sides of the rectangle, and make another circle.

You now have a drawing that looks somewhat like a figure 8. Connect the circles with two curved lines according to the measurements shown in A. The pattern now looks like a very large peanut. Cut out this pattern and lay it on the soft leather close to the edge. Then trace around it with a pencil. Now move the pattern over beside the one just traced, and outline it again. Repeat this until you have drawn four such outlines.

B shows how best to make use of a small piece

of leather for two double balls and for the thongs that will connect the double balls. Notice carefully how to draw the spirals that will be the thongs. Each thong is one inch wide at the wider part and ½ inch wide at the narrow part. The wide part is 5 inches long.

The four ball covers and the two spiral sections that make the thongs are next cut out carefully with a pair of scissors. Cut carefully along the lines making the spiral. The spiral cuts will stretch out to form a nice, straight thong.

Tie a knot in the thong just above the broad

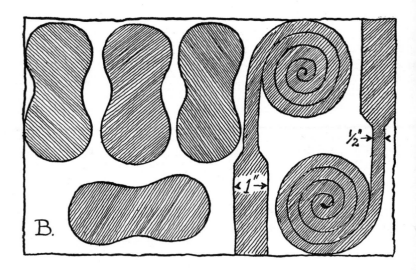

end, as in C. Then place the thong between two cover sections, as in D, and start sewing the sections together, beginning at one end. When you have stitched halfway up each side of the bottom ball, begin stuffing it. Cotton makes good stuffing; you can tamp it down firmly with the eraser end of your pencil. Remember to lay plenty of cotton all along the thong, in order to keep the thong in the middle of the stuffing. Stuff the balls bit by bit, working from one end to the other, and stitch up the sides as you go until the first double ball is finished. See E.

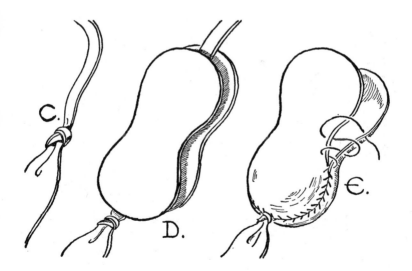

C.

D.

E.

The two leather thongs must now be joined together. With the knife, slit the narrow ends as in F. The shaded thong is the one fastened to the first double ball. Start the splice by passing 2 through 1, as in G. Then pass the broad end of 2 through its own slit, H.

Pull 1 up tight and fold its end over, as in

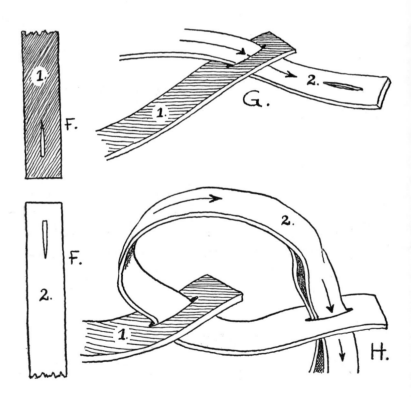

I, completing the splice by pulling the ends together, as in J.

Then tie a knot above the broad end of 2, as in K, and complete the second double ball, as in D and E.

When you have finished, wrap strong string around the narrow section between the upper

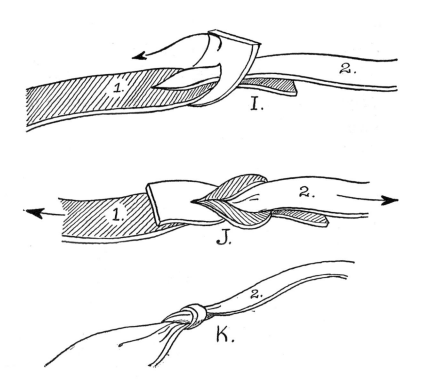

and lower half of each double ball, as in M and N. Colored string, or cord, or ribbon—if you have some—improves the looks of the double ball.

Finally, cut a few thin fringes into the broad end of each thong, below the knot, as in L.

Now you are ready to make the playing stick, O. From a green sapling cut a branch about 20 inches long and 1 inch thick. Bend the tip down, slowly, in order not to snap it, and then tie it to keep it bent, as in P. Let the branch dry out for a day or two. Then when you take off the string, the branch will stay bent.

If you cannot find a sapling, use a piece of plywood ¾ inch thick. Make a paper pattern first, following Q, and trace it on the wood. Cut out the stick with a coping saw, and sandpaper the edges until they are smooth and round.

Two 6-inch branches or dowels will do for scoring sticks. If you use small branches, scrape the bark from one of them with a pocketknife, so that you may tell them apart. If you use dowels, paint one yellow and the other red.

Before you play, set up two goals at opposite

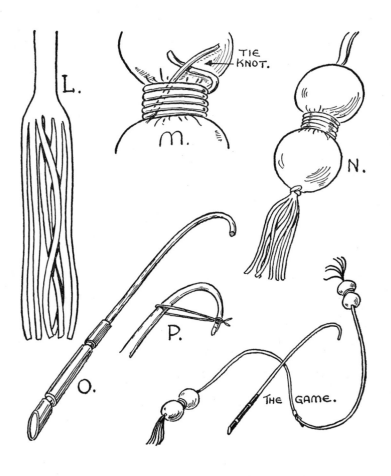

L.

TIE KNOT.

M.

N.

O.

P.

THE GAME.

Q.

1 INCH SQUARES.

ends of the field. A row of stones six feet long will do. Extra stones should be piled at each end. When your team becomes good at the game, set up goal posts, about six feet high and six feet apart, with a crossbar in between. Then you can make your goals in the true Indian manner by making the double balls catch on the crossbar.

Place the scoring sticks on the ground about 12 inches apart. As a team makes a goal, its scoring stick is moved up one inch toward the other stick. The inning is then over, and the teams must face off again in the center of the field. When the sticks meet, the team whose stick has been moved the farthest is the winner.

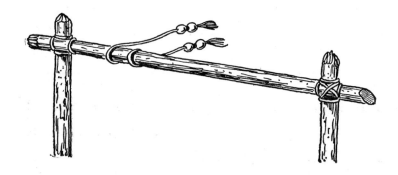

10

Toss and Catch

THIS game is a favorite of the Eskimos of Labrador. It is a convenient game, because you can carry it along with you when you travel. Eskimos often carve the pieces out of ivory. Since ivory is both hard to find and hard to carve, we will substitute wood for our game. This, however, still keeps it an Indian game, for the Sioux and Cheyenne Indians used wood.

The materials you will need are few.

One dowel stick 1 inch in diameter and 10 inches long.

One dowel stick $\frac{1}{4}$ inch in diameter and 8 inches long.

One piece of white pine wood, 3 by 5 inches and $\frac{1}{4}$ inch thick.

One $\frac{3}{8}$-inch drill.

One $\frac{1}{4}$-inch drill.

One strong cord, 18 inches long.

Water colors and brush.

Coping saw.

Sharp knife.

Sandpaper, rough and fine.

Vise.

To make the handle and the pointed catcher, place the 10-inch dowel stick in a vise, and into one end of the stick drill a $\frac{1}{4}$-inch hole about 2 inches deep. See A.

Next cover the lower two inches of the 8-inch dowel with glue, and insert this end into the hole just drilled. See B.

While the glue is drying, square off a piece of paper to the dimensions shown in C, and within

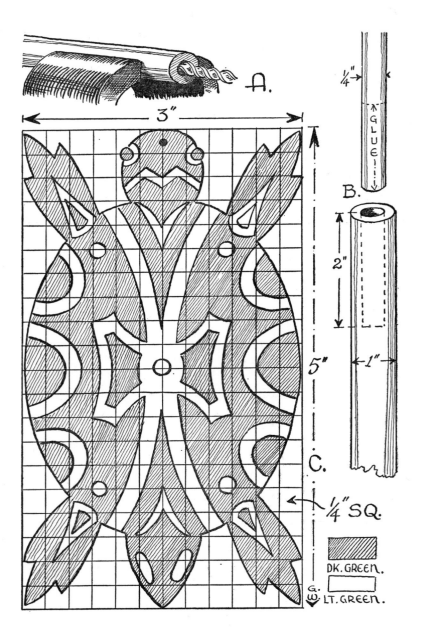

A.

3"

5"

B.

¼"

GLUE

2"

1"

C.

¼" SQ.

DK. GREEN.

LT. GREEN.

G.
W.

those squares draw the outline of the turtle and also the design on its shell. Cut out a paper pattern and trace the turtle outline on the 3-by-5-inch piece of pine wood. Cut the turtle out with the coping saw.

With the ⅜-inch drill make one hole in the middle of the turtle's back, and with the same drill make four more holes in the shell, directly behind each of the four legs.

Make a smaller hole, using a thin nail or a small awl, in the turtle's head between the eyes to hold the cord.

Paint the entire turtle light green, and when it is dry place your drawing pattern on the turtle again, and trace on the design. Then fill in the shaded design in the drawing with a dark green.

The glue has now dried on the handle, and we can taper the thinner dowel. This is done by sandpapering it from a little below the center out to the tip.

To prevent the friction caused by rubbing from burning your hand as you work, place the sand-

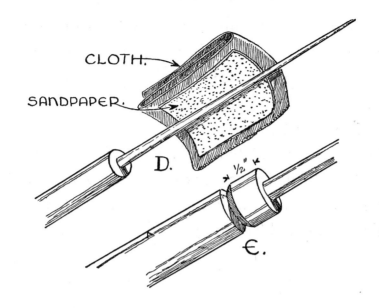

CLOTH.

SANDPAPER.

D.

½"

E.

paper face up on a piece of folded cloth held in your hand. Wrap cloth and sandpaper around the dowel, and give the rod a vigorous rubbing. Use the roughest sandpaper first, and keep working toward the tip so that the rod will taper gradually. When the rod looks like D, sand it smooth with a fine grade of sandpaper.

Next cut a groove all around the thicker rod, as in E, about ½ inch below the end where the two rods join.

Now take the cord. Tie one end to the head of the turtle and the other end to the groove in the handle, making the whole project look like F.

The object of the turtle game is to catch the turtle on the pointed stick. Hold the handle so that the turtle hangs free on the cord. Then, with a slight upward swing of the hand, toss the turtle into the air. Try to make the stick go through

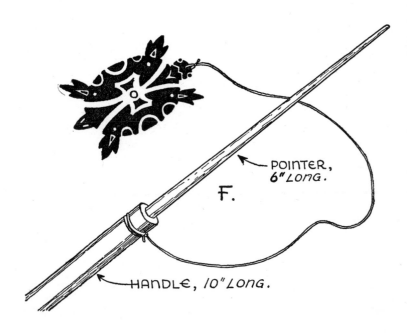

POINTER, 6" LONG.

F.

HANDLE, 10" LONG.

one of the holes on the turtle's back, and score as follows:

Center hole—50 points.
Right front leg—40.
Left front leg—30.
Right hind leg—20.
Left hind leg—10.

Each player should have five tosses per turn. The second toss and catch game, shown in G and H, is made with the following materials:

A piece of plywood, 3½ inches by 6 inches.

Dowel rod, ¾ inch in diameter, 6 inches long.

A curtain ring, 2 inches in diameter, from five-and-ten.

Strong cord, 18 inches long.

Two short screws.

An awl, 2 inches long.

Coping saw.

Water colors and brush.

Draw the pattern (see G) on squared-off paper. Cut out the paper pattern, trace it on the plywood, and cut it out with the coping saw. With an awl make a small hole in the top of the shield.

The handle is a dowel rod, ¾ inch in diameter and 6 inches long. Two inches from one end of the handle make a cut that is ⅜ inch deep, using the coping saw. Now saw straight down from the top of the handle to this cut, making a flat recess, as in I. Set the shield and horns into this recess and fasten the piece with the two short screws, as shown in J.

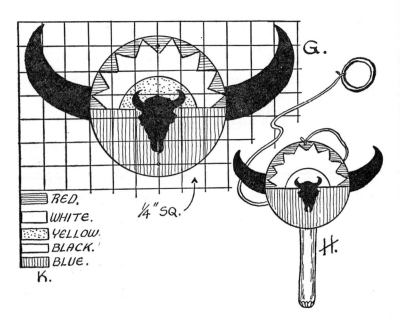

G.

RED.
WHITE.
YELLOW.
BLACK.
BLUE.
K.

¼" SQ.

H.

Tie one end of the 18-inch cord to the ring and the other through the small hole in the top of the shield.

Paint the shield and horns with water colors, as indicated in K.

The ring toss is only for amusement and does not call for a score. When you become skillful at catching the ring on one of the horns, add another cord and ring to the handle. Try to catch both rings at the same time, one on each horn, as in L.

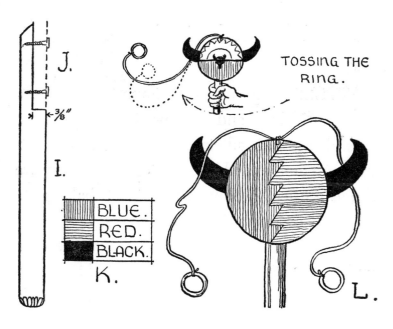

TOSSING THE RING.

J.

←⅜″

I.

| BLUE. |
| RED. |
| BLACK. |

K.

L.

11

Indian Rattles

RATTLES were of great importance to the American Indian, and they used many different types of rattles. Medicine men shook special rattles in ceremonies and healing rituals. Rattles were used as musical instruments during tribal dances and as an accompaniment to singers.

Indian rattles were made from any one of a number of materials, including buffalo horns, turtle shells, gourds, rawhide, and elm or birch bark.

In more recent times, Indians have even used tin cans to make their rattles.

Here are directions for making three rattles: the first out of a tin can, the second out of a gourd, and the third out of a horn.

For the tin-can rattle you need the following:

A large-size evaporated-milk can.

Two round toothpicks.

One 10-inch dowel stick, ½ inch in diameter.

A small can of white or blue flat oil paint.

A can opener.

A ⅛-inch drill.

One small, flat brush.

Dark blue, red, and yellow water colors in small jars.

A small water-color paintbrush.

To drain the contents of the can, punch a hole in the top with the can opener. Be careful to make the hole as near the center as possible, rather than on the side. Turn the can upside down over a bowl and make a similar hole in the other end. Let the contents drain into the bowl. Then rinse the can thoroughly with cold water and remove all paper wrapping.

To make the handle, B, bore a hole with the drill near one end of the dowel stick. Insert one of the toothpicks, and break off the toothpick ends so that they protrude, as in B.

With the point of the can opener enlarge the hole in the top of the can. Then push the dowel stick through the top hole and out through the bottom hole of the can. Push the can up along the dowel until the top of the can is flush with the toothpick, as in A.

Mark the dowel where it comes out through the bottom of the can. Take the can off and drill a hole through the dowel at the mark you have made. When the toothpick is put through this hole, it will be at a right angle to the toothpick at the top. See C.

Put a few pebbles inside the can and reinsert the dowel. Push the can up to the top toothpick. Fasten the second toothpick through the lower hole, and snip off the ends as before. Now the can is held securely in place.

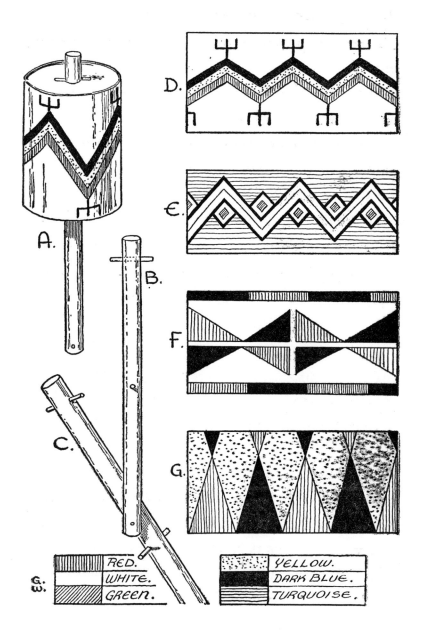

A.

B.

C.

D.

E.

F.

G.

G.
W.

	RED.
	WHITE.
	GREEN.

	YELLOW.
	DARK BLUE.
	TURQUOISE.

The designs shown in D through G can now be painted on the can. First paint the entire can with a coat of flat white or light-blue oil paint. When the oil paint is dry, lightly sketch in the design, and then paint it with water or poster colors. Let the water colors dry and then cover the can with clear varnish.

To make the gourd rattle, marked H, you will need the following:

One large gourd. This may be bought at a florist shop.

One 10-inch dowel stick, ½ inch in diameter.

Two round toothpicks.

Turquoise, yellow, and red water colors.

A water-color brush.

A ⅛-inch drill.

A pocketknife.

With the knife, cut a neat hole, ½ inch in diameter, in the top of the gourd. Cut a similar hole in the bottom of the gourd. Now take some stiff wire, such as part of a coat hanger, and bend the end over. With this end, scrape all the dry seeds out of the gourd.

To fasten the gourd on the dowel-stick handle, follow the directions for making the tin-can rattle. Put a few pebbles inside the gourd, run the handle through it, and insert the lower toothpick to hold it in place.

This type of rattle is favored by the Indians of the Southwest, and therefore it would be appropriate to paint on it designs used in this region. Such designs are shown in the diagrams I, J, K, L, and M. Paint them directly onto the gourd, in brilliant turquoise, yellow, and red. No varnish should be used.

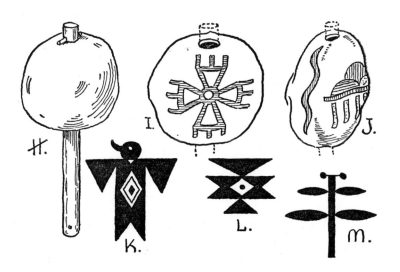

The horn rattle is more complicated to make, but it is typically Indian, and the completed result will well repay the work of making it. Most Plains Indians used horn rattles, and they were also popular with the early Iroquois.

You will need the following to make the horn rattle, P:

One cow horn (or two if you wish to make a set). Your local butcher might get them for you.

One dowel stick, 12 inches long and ¾ inch in diameter.

One piece of wood about ⅜ inch thick. The ends of a small crate, obtainable at a grocery store, can be used.

A small box of brass-headed upholstery nails.

One toothpick.

An ice pick.

A piece of broken glass.

A hammer.

A coping saw.

Wax polish.

First scrape the rough outer surface of the cow horn with the piece of glass until it is smooth.

Then make a straight cut with the coping saw through the broad end of the cow horn. See N. Measure off six inches from this cut edge and cut through the horn again at the same angle.

Now take the piece of horn you have just cut off and lay the broad end on the piece of wood. With a long, sharp pencil, reach into the horn and trace on the wood the outline of the inner rim. See O. Then turn the horn on its narrow end

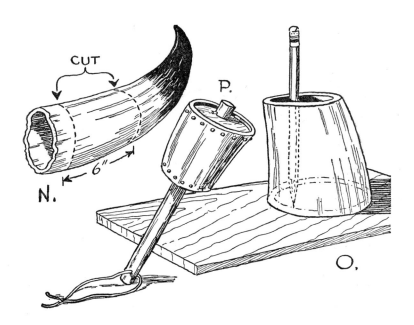

and make a tracing of that inner rim. Leave about half an inch between the tracings. Saw the board apart between the tracings. Now cut out the two pieces with the coping saw. Cut these pieces very carefully, as they must fit exactly into the ends of the horn.

Drill a ½-inch hole in the center of each piece of wood. Then drill an evenly spaced row of holes around the edges of the horn, as in Q.

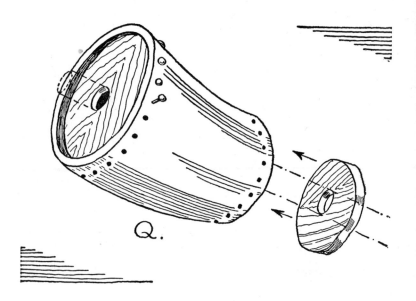

Q.

Now set the larger wood section into the larger end of the horn, and hammer the upholstery nails through the holes and into the wood. See Q. Drop 8 or 10 pebbles into the horn. Fasten the smaller wood section into the smaller end of the horn.

To make the handle, measure off 6½ inches from one end of the dowel stick. Cut a fine groove with the coping saw around the stick at this point. With the knife, whittle away the upper end, as

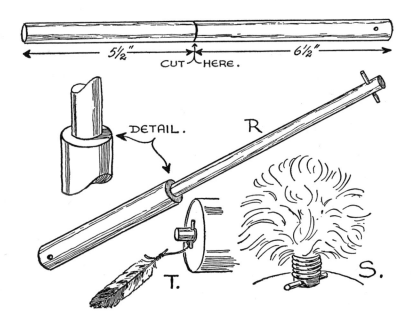

in R, leaving the grip the original thickness. The upper end of the handle must fit firmly into the holes drilled into the wood ends.

Slip the horn down over the handle until it comes to rest upon the broader part of the handle. A small hole is then drilled into the handle just above the top of the horn, and the toothpick is set in, as in the other handles.

The protruding tip on any of the rattles may be decorated by tying some small plumes or feathers around it, as indicated in S. A single large feather can be fastened to the tip, as shown in T.

A thong, for hanging the rattle from your wrist or on the wall, can be added by drilling a small hole near the bottom of the handle, and then knotting in a cord or thong of leather or buckskin.

12

Owner Sticks

MANY years ago, it was customary for the Crow
Indians of Montana to use owner sticks to iden-
tify their personal belongings. Owner sticks were
slender rods about 2 feet long, with decorations
that were symbolic of the person to whom they
belonged. A Crow brave whose name was Black
Buffalo, for instance, cut a small piece of rawhide
in the shape of a buffalo, blackened it with char-
coal, and fastened it to a small crosspiece at the
top of his owner stick. Another brave, Red Plume,
tied several red feathers to a hoop on his stick.

When Black Buffalo or Red Plume gathered a pile of dry branches for use in a fire pit, he would mark them as his own by driving his owner stick into the ground beside the pile. Then no other Indian could claim the branches. In the same way a deer hide or buffalo skin pegged to the ground to dry would be perfectly safe if it was guarded by an owner stick.

Each family had its own design for owner sticks, and a number of duplicates were always made, as several sticks were sometimes used at the same time by a family or by a person.

Such owner sticks are interesting to make, and they can be useful as well. They make good markers for several of the games described in this book. If you are interested in camping, select a design as your own and take an owner stick with you on a camping trip. You can set it in the ground at the foot of your sleeping bag or put it beside your camping gear.

Groups in summer camps can make owner sticks with unit designs, each cabin group making its own stick and placing it in front of the cabin. Each cabin group may make duplicate sticks, just as the Indians did. At the council fire or at other gatherings, each member can then carry his own stick, indicating the group to which he belongs.

Three different owner sticks are shown in the illustrations. You can make any one of them with the materials listed below. Willow sticks may be hard to find except in the country. Dowel rods may take their place.

You will need the following:

One willow stick or dowel rod, 24 inches long and ½ inch thick.

One willow stick or dowel rod, 7½ inches long and ¼ inch thick.

Two pieces of fur, soft leather, or stout cloth: the first, about 9 inches by 1¾ inches; the second, 7½ inches by 1¾ inches.

A scrap piece of sole leather or plywood about 6 inches square.

Several bunches of horsehair or colored yarn, each about 12 inches long.

Colored ribbon, in 2 or 3 different colors.

Chicken or turkey feathers.

Glue.

Needle and thread.

To make the owner stick shown in A, take the longer dowel and drill a ¼-inch hole 6 inches from the top. Into the hole insert the 7½-inch dowel to make a crosspiece. The ends should extend an equal distance on each side.

Cut a scrap of fur, cloth, or leather; fit it snugly around the large dowel, and sew it in place, as shown in D. Brightly colored yarn, wrapped around this at top and bottom, will add color.

The hoop fastened to the stick at the intersection is made from a piece of basket-weaving material. Soak it first in hot water for an hour or two to make it more pliable. Then bend it slowly to form a loop, and tie it to the owner stick at each side of the crossbar. See A and B.

Take the horsehair or colored yarn and make four small bunches of 12-inch strands. Fold each bunch over a cord, wind yarn around it, and tie

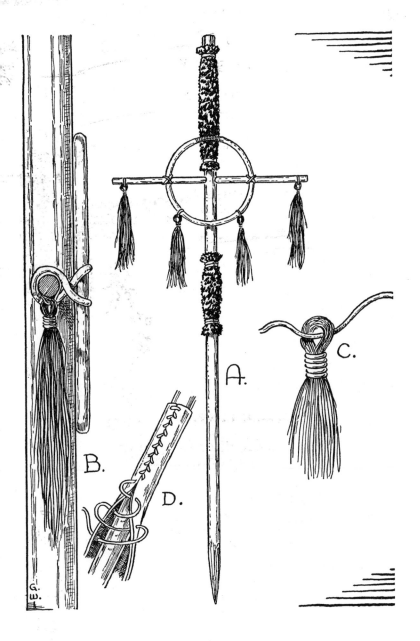

A.

B.

C.

D.

G.
W.

it fast, as in C. Tie the bunches to the owner stick, as in A.

Cut a small groove at each end of the crossbar and on either side of the hoop so that the bunches will not slip, once you have tied them on. See A, and also B for the side view.

Some owner sticks displayed the totem of the head of the family. E shows the totem on the owner stick used by Red Eagle.

To make this owner stick, first make the crossbar as described for the owner stick in A. Then sew a piece of colored cloth around the stick, above and below the crossbar. It should extend about 8 inches below the crossbar. Wrap the cloth with yarn of a different color, for contrast.

Now drill a small hole into the top of the upright. Dip a short feather in glue and set it into the hole. If you have a plume, set it in with the first feather, as in F.

You may wish to select your own Indian name and make a totem to fit it. In the back of the author's book, *Indian Sign Language,* you will find a list of Indian names and their totems.

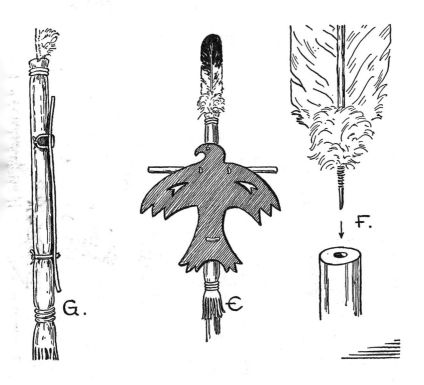

The totem in E is cut from a piece of sole leather; or it may be cut from ¼-inch plywood with a coping saw. Drill three pairs of small holes through the totem so that rawhide or twine may be passed through, as shown in E. Then tie the totem to the crossbar, as shown in G.

To make the third owner stick shown in H, begin by making a crossbar as you did for the other sticks. However, be sure to sew and wrap the leather or cloth to the upright before you insert the crossbar. Set plumes or small feathers into a hole drilled at the top of the upright. Cut fringes at the top and bottom edges of the wrapping. Make the top fringe 1½ inches long and the bottom fringe 3 inches long.

Cut two thin strips of soft leather or felt, 8 inches long and ½ inch wide. Fold the top end of each strip over the crossbar and tie it on, as in I. Then cut three fringes at the bottom, and shorten the outer fringes, as in I. Tie small plumes or short feathers to the ends of the fringes, as in J.

For outdoor use, sharpen the lower ends to a point with a pocketknife.

For further owner-stick designs and for more detailed information on their use, read the chapter "Owner Sticks," in the author's book, *The Indian's Secret World.*

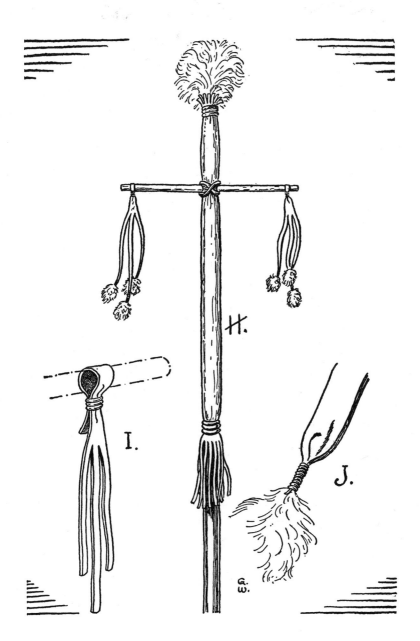

H.

I.

J.

13

The Pump Drill

THE pump drill was a tool widely used by many Indian tribes. The Iroquois used it to drill holes in their wampum, the Navaho to drill holes in turquoise beads. Thus pierced, the beads or wampum could be strung. Other tribes fitted the drill with points, or bits, of various sizes for drilling into wood and pipestone.

A pump drill will help you to make several of the articles described in this book, and other things as well. In this book, wherever a small hand drill is mentioned, the pump drill can take its place. It can be made at little cost.

You will need the following materials:

One piece of plywood, 6½ inches square and ⅜ inch thick.

One piece of plywood, 8 inches long, 1⅛ inches wide, and ¼ inch thick.

One dowel rod, 12 inches long and ½ inch in diameter.

An 18-inch length of strong, smooth string.

A ½-inch bit.

A ⅝-inch bit.

A 1½-inch brad.

A hand drill with a ⅛-inch bit.

A coping saw.

On the square piece of plywood draw a 6-inch circle, following the method used in making the circles on the target for corncob darts. (See Chapter 4.) Use a piece of string 3 inches long. Drill a hole with the ½-inch bit in the center of this circle. Cut out the circle with the coping saw. Now you have made the flywheel shown in A.

In the center of the 8-inch plywood strip, B,

drill a hole with the ⅝-inch bit. Round off the corners of the strip, as in B, and with the ⅛-inch hand drill bore a hole at each end of the strip, as in B.

With the hand drill bore a hole through one end of the dowel, ½ inch from the tip. Now drive the 1½-inch brad about half an inch into the center of the other end of the dowel. Make sure the brad goes in straight. Then file off the head of the brad, making a sharp point for drilling.

The flywheel, A, fits onto the dowel 3 inches from the bottom, as in E. It must fit snugly, so it might be wise to coat the inside of the hole in the wheel with a little glue before you put the wheel on. Now pass the 18-inch length of string through the upper hole in the dowel and make two even ends. Slip the bar, B, over the dowel and tie the ends of the string through the small holes in the bar. You should knot the ends so that the bar hangs freely, 1 inch above the flywheel. See C, and the dotted lines in E.

The pump drill is now ready for use.

Set the brad point on the spot to be drilled.

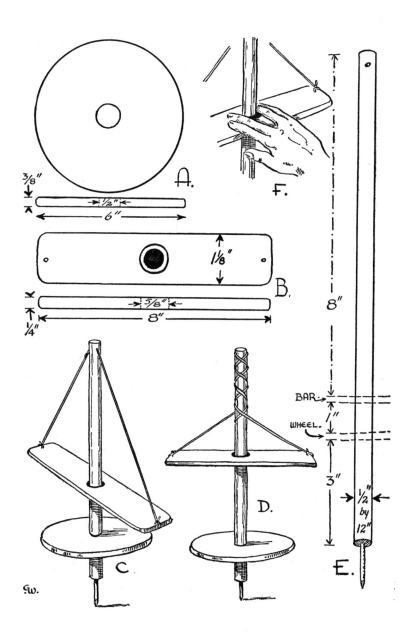

3/8"

1/2"

6"

A.

1 1/8"

5/8"

8"

1/4"

B.

C.

D.

Gw.

F.

8"

BAR.

WHEEL.

1"

3"

1/2"
by
12"

E.

Now spin the bar. The string will twist itself upward around the dowel, raising the bar to the position shown in D. Now put your fingers on the bar and press gently. As the string unwinds, the wheel spins and starts the drilling. See F.

Just as the string unwinds completely, release the pressure. The flywheel will keep spinning long enough to rewind the string and raise the bar again. Rest your fingers on the bar without pressure until the string is rewound, then press down once more.

It is the flywheel's momentum, and not the pressure of your fingers, that keeps the drill spinning. Thus you need press only hard enough to start the flywheel each time the bar reaches the top, as in D. Practice making holes in scraps of wood until you get the feel of the drill; then you will know exactly how much pressure is needed.

For a pump drill that makes larger holes, a small nail may be used in place of the brad. The flywheel should then be made of heavier stock, to add weight. Use ½-inch to ⅝-inch plywood instead of the ⅜-inch thickness.

14

Hopi Kachinas

THE carving of the Hopi kachinas is a project for a more advanced craftsman.

A few kachinas described here are examples of the more than two hundred such figures used in the ceremonies of the Hopi Indians in the Southwest. To the Hopi these figures represent everything in nature, from rain clouds and rain to beans, birds, and animals. During the ceremonial dances, the men of the villages dress in brightly colored costumes and masks, some of which are reproduced in these carved kachinas.

There is no standard size for these figures; but, as a starter, work on one not less than six inches tall. A figure smaller than that would be more difficult to work on.

The tools and materials are these:

One block of white pine 6 inches long, 3½ inches wide, and 3½ inches thick.

A few round, pointed toothpicks.

Some small feathers.

Tube of glue.

Small jars of poster colors in red, yellow, light blue, black, white, and brick red.

Small piece of thin, stiff white cardboard.

Piece of balsa wood, 2 by 5 inches and ¾ of an inch thick.

Coping saw.

Fine sandpaper.

A *sharp* pocketknife with a small blade. Keep a small sharpening stone handy so that the blade can be whetted often.

On the wood block lay out in pencil a rough outline of the three-quarter view of the figure, as shown in A. With the coping saw, cut away the shaded portions, first from the front, then from the sides. Take care that the saw blade is held straight when you cut the feet, or they will not be the same size. With the point of the pocket-knife, cut away the straight-sided section between the arms, hands, and body, so that you will have a rough figure like the one in B.

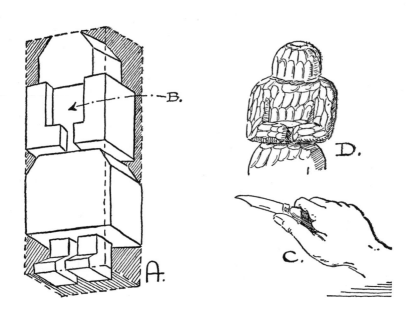

To have full control of the knife when carving, hold the wood in the left hand, and the handle of the knife in the right. Then, as in C, place your thumb on the back edge of the small knife blade and apply a slight pressure with the thumb, as you carve away section after section of the wood. This is better than forcing the knife with the hand, as in this way the knife will stop as soon as the pressure of the thumb ceases.

The next step is to carve away all the angular edges, cutting gradually and a little at a time. See D. Study E and F carefully. They show the shape of the kachina plus the headdress, or *tableta*.

As the arms begin to take shape, the chest and back are slightly rounded, as in F, allowing the mask to extend a bit, front and back.

The kilt curves inward at the waist but keeps its flare at the bottom all the way around.

Shape the feet carefully with the knife so that the upper part of the foot is rounded at the ankle and the legs taper toward this point. Make sure that the soles of the feet are perfectly even so

E.

that the kachina will stand upright by itself.

When the whole figure has been shaped up, sandpaper the entire surface to remove all traces of knife marks.

One more step comes before the painting starts, and that is to cut the slit into the mask, as shown in H. This slit is a cut made with the coping saw; into it the headdress, J, is later fitted.

The kachina is now ready for painting. On the carved figure draw the lines separating the colors. Then, starting with the lightest color first, fill in the sections with the poster colors, following the color chart, K.

E, F, and H show front and side views of the mask, and G shows the back view. The yellow covering the chest of the figure in the front view also extends down the back.

Figure I shows the full view of the kilt and sash design and their colors.

The flat nose is cut from a tiny sliver of wood and is glued to the front center of the mask.

When the colors are dry, place the pattern of the kachina headdress on the thin, stiff piece of

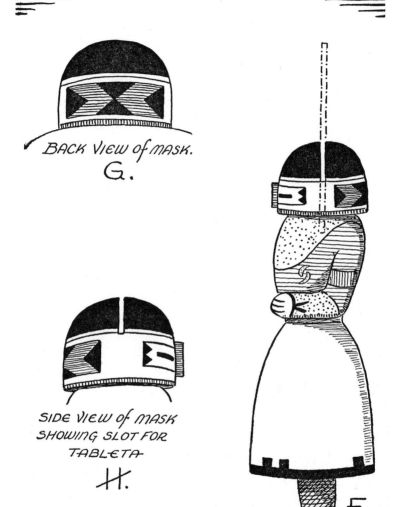

BACK VIEW of MASK.
G.

SIDE VIEW of MASK
SHOWING SLOT FOR
TABLETA
H.

F.

G. W.

cardboard and, with a pointed pencil, draw the curve. From the bottom of this curve measure off ¾ of an inch on each side, and with this as a guide, draw the step-up outline. See J.

Within this outline draw the design. The front of the headdress is shown in E, and the back in J. Draw the front first; then with the knife point cut out the headdress and then draw in the back. Be sure not to cut out the inner section that is marked in J: *Set into slot*. This is the piece that

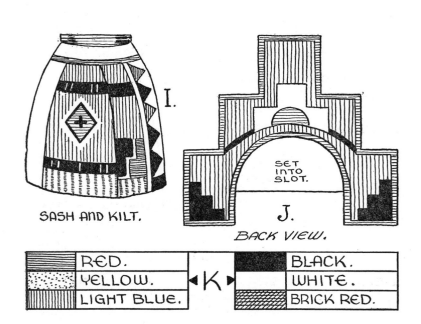

SASH AND KILT.

J.

BACK VIEW.

	RED.	◄ K ►		BLACK.	
	YELLOW.			WHITE.	
	LIGHT BLUE.			BRICK RED.	

holds the headdress in place when it is set into the slot cut in the mask.

Drill two small holes on a slant in the back of the mask and insert a small feather in each so that they extend beyond the headdress. Now this Niman, or Home-going Kachina, is finished.

Do not varnish any of the kachinas. They look more authentic when left in the flat colors.

The companion kachina, shown in 1 and 2, is to be laid out on a block of wood in the same dimensions and in the same way as the one just described. Here the figure has a ruff, or collar, around its neck. This must be added in drawing it. The same careful method of carving is to be followed.

When the kachina has been cut and sanded, the two protruding ears, shown in 3, are cut with the saw from a small piece of the ¾-inch balsa wood. Into the flat ends of these two ears set two pointed pieces from a toothpick, and drill corresponding holes into the sides of the mask. Drop a little glue on each toothpick tip and insert the ears into the mask. See 1 and 4.

1.

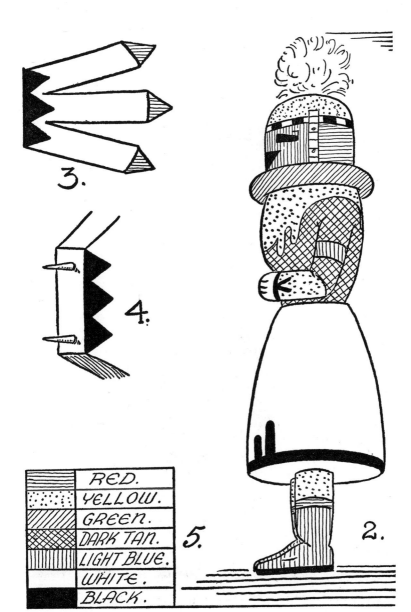

3.

4.

	RED.
	YELLOW.
	GREEN.
	DARK TAN.
	LIGHT BLUE.
	WHITE.
	BLACK.

5.

2.

The colorings for this kachina are shown in 5. The top of the mask is decorated with plumes.

Still another kachina can be made with the same body as number 1, but with the mask shown in 8. In the front of the mask drill a ¼-inch hole into which a ¼-inch dowel stick, 1 inch long, is inserted and held with a little glue. This is a Warrior Kachina.

The Silent Kachina, number 6, is carved as if it had a shawl or mantle over its shoulders. Figure 6 shows that the shawl is carved to turn back at the sides, showing the kilt. The colors for this figure are the same as those given in 5, except that in this case the black shown in the mantle drawing should be painted green.

To change the Silent Kachina into a Crowbride Kachina, all that is necessary is to carve the head in 9 on the shoulders of 6 and 7.

Feathers are set into holes drilled into the back of the mask of 6, and small downy feathers are glued on top of the mask as in 9.

On top of the mask in 8, two small feathers are placed. These are first tied together near the

base with thin thread. Then the tied part is fastened to the top of the mask with glue.

Other kachina designs may be obtained from books in your library. After you have carved the kachinas described here, you will be able to make copies of others.

Standing on a bookcase, or hanging on your wall, the kachinas are decorative. To make them functional as well, mount two, as shown in C, to be used as book ends. They can be either twins or different kachinas.

Make the uprights, A, from ⅜-inch plywood, and the base, B, from ½- to ⅝-inch pine. Cut and paint as indicated, and screw the uprights to the bases. Then glue the kachinas to the bases as shown in C.

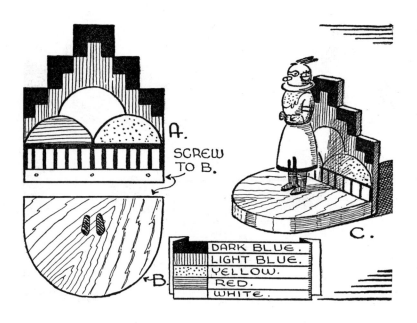

A.
SCREW TO B.

DARK BLUE.
LIGHT BLUE.
YELLOW.
RED.
WHITE.

B.

C.

Another functional use for the kachinas is to use them on an outdoor sign. Here, the figures must be fairly large, depending upon the size of the sign.

The sign suggested in A should be made from a strip of 5-ply marine, or exterior, plywood, and the kachinas must be carved to fit as shown.

For this sign, the *tabletas* are cut out as part of the signboard itself, as shown in B. The kachinas are carved with flat backs, as in C.

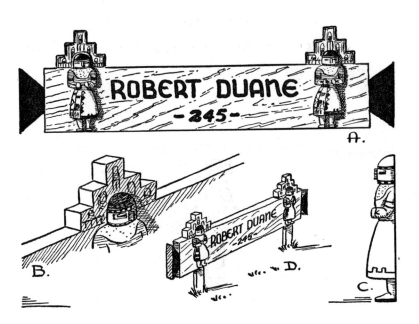

The head mask of the kachina is then placed in the lower center of the *tableta;* the soles of the feet are even with the lower edge of the signboard. Then the kachinas are fastened to the sign with screws from the back.

A sign 24 inches long and 8 inches wide with a 3-inch *tableta* at each end will serve as a name and house number plate, to be placed either at one side of the door or above it. A sign made on larger dimensions may be used as a lawn marker, as suggested in D.

Screw the legs to the sign back of the kachinas, making them long enough to reach well into the ground for stability.

ROBERT HOFSINDE was born in Denmark and received his art training at the famous Royal Art Academy of Copenhagen. He came to the United States as a young man and has lived here ever since.

While trapping in the Minnesota forests, he saved the life of a Chippewa Indian boy who had broken his leg. In token of their gratitude, the Chippewas made Mr. Hofsinde a blood brother of their tribe, giving him the name of Gray-Wolf in an ancient ceremony that mingled his blood with theirs. This was the beginning of his interest in the culture of the American Indian.

Over the years, Mr. Hofsinde has contributed more than 300 craft articles to the leading magazines in this field, including *Popular Science* and *Popular Mechanics*. His articles on Indian life, illustrated by himself, have appeared in many periodicals both here and abroad. He has also been director of Indian crafts and lore in several summer camps and has directed leadership courses for camp counselors.

He now lives in Monroe, New York, where he is curator of the Plume Indian Museum.